AF575206

How to Teach Joy

A Simple Guide to Nurturing a Child's Development

Written by
Teacher Joy

Illustrated by
Brooke Ivey

How to Teach Joy
A Simple Guide to Nurturing
A Child's Development
Published by
Saved By Story Publishing, LLC
Prescott, AZ

www.SavedByStory.house

Illustrations by Brooke Ivey
Cover by Alyssa Noelle Coelho
Interior Design by Dawn Teagarden

ISBN: 978-1-961336-08-7

Printed in the United States of America

www.SavedByStory.house

To my fantastic sons
who grew up to be amazing men,
and the mentors I've had along the way.

Teacher Joy

To my dogs, Nebbia and Onyx.
Thanks for the constant cuddles, comedic relief,
and countless distractions you offered throughout my work on this project.
Hope that the puppy in this book can tickle all you dog lovers out there.

Brooke Ivey

Teacher Joy Brooke Ivey

INTRODUCTION

There I sat at the kitchen table, feeling like an utter failure. Depressed and exhausted, I just couldn't keep up.

How am I ever going to get it all done? I wondered as I surveyed my space and tried to gather enough energy for the next task.

The dishes were piled high, as I only had enough time to wash the ones I needed to make the next meal. Over time, the bottom of the pile that got no attention had begun to smell. I was nineteen years old, a student of child development at the local college, and trying to step back into the workforce after having my second baby who knew one thing really well—how to scream. He was colicky, uncomfortable, and downright mad at the world. Nursing was an absolute fail. He would only eat a little bit and then scream in pain and stop eating. He wasn't thriving, and my milk supply was diminishing rapidly. The first five months of his life had been hard on all of us.

I tried everything anyone told me, including his doctor, and read every book I could to give me some insight on how to fix this clearly broken baby. Thank goodness my two-year-old was easy-going because this little guy took every ounce of energy I had... and then some.

My depression grew deeper and darker each day. I was losing sleep and gaining weight. It felt like I was always nursing or burping, which left little time for taking a shower or combing out my knotty hair.

Losing myself completely, there eventually came a moment when I felt like my children would be better off without me. My postpartum depression took me to a dark place that I couldn't get out of alone, as it had triggered many old traumas that had not been addressed or healed. When I started therapy, the psychiatrist prescribed me medication, but it was not the answer for me. In fact, my reaction to the antidepressants only intensified my emotions and I was not only contemplating suicide—I was making a plan.

Eventually, I found a therapist who listened to my whole story and told me to stop taking the antidepressants and face my traumas instead. We started talking about the reality of postpartum depression and how to find some hope. Remembering that my happiness was tied to my passion, I knew I needed to find my way back to the early education classroom.

Everything I've been learning in my child development classes isn't working with you just yet...

I sighed as I looked down into the nearly-purple face of my second child screaming in my arms.

I pulled him closer and promised, "Mommy is going to figure it out, baby boy. We're going to figure out what it is you need to be happy and healthy."

I KNOW IT'S NOT JUST ME

If you are reading this book, it's likely because you are a new or seasoned parent, caregiver, or educator who feels like I did all those years ago.

Maybe you're a new mother, absolutely in love with your baby and terrified you're going to fail. You have big dreams for them—their health, happiness, and future. And yet, even with all the unsolicited advice from other moms, you move through your day feeling like you're missing something. The initial stress of feeding, changing diapers, and naps has been replaced by the nagging feeling that you could be doing more to help them learn, grow, and thrive.

So, in between the endless cycles of laundry, dishes, and burning dinners, you go online to find answers to questions about your child's development and quickly find yourself spiraling emotionally, comparing yourself to other moms, creating an endless list of to-dos. By the time your partner or family members arrive at the end of the day, you're frazzled and exhausted, not just from the effort required to keep a human alive but from wondering if you're cut out to be a mom at all. Worse yet, you pretend that everything is just fine because "new moms should just know what to do, right?"

Perhaps you are one of the caregivers in this new mom's life and have no idea how to support her with her big goals for raising a happy, healthy child.

Or maybe you are an early educator working with little ones and you want to do more than babysit or watch the children play. You know you could be doing more to help them learn the skills they will need to thrive in school and life, and you know the time is now. You just don't know the how and, frankly, in the state early education is in right now, you may not even know the why. Maybe you're looking for more information about what's happening naturally in the bodies, minds, hearts, and souls of the little ones, so that you can more easily come alongside them and nurture it all.

Whether you are a parent, caregiver, or educator, I believe the insights and skills I've placed in the following pages will answer your questions, give you ways to practically apply what you are learning, and help you build that confidence in your ability to really show up and nurture the children in your life.

DETERMINED TO DO IT BETTER

When my first son was born, I was seventeen years old and basically on my own. I'll save you all the horrible details, but let's just say my family wasn't supportive of my decision to keep my baby and my boyfriend wasn't exactly father material.

My childhood was full of a lot of uncertainty and false impressions. I'm sure my parents were doing the best they could with what they had at the time, but it wasn't enough to protect me from the impact of the little and big traumas that occurred.

By the time my little guy came into the world, the cracks were beginning to show. Socially, I was alone and abandoned by my family and my friends. Emotionally, I was insecure and full of self-loathing, desperate to be happy. Cognitively, I knew I didn't think or learn like others, and I wondered if something was wrong with me and why no one seemed to care enough to tell me. Creatively, I was stunted and felt I wasn't allowed to play or be myself. It was difficult to access my imagination and use it to create a new possibility. Physically, I was a wreck, suffering from anorexia and depression.

In other words, I had no idea how to care for my own well-being, much less a defenseless baby. But, despite all of it, I felt determined that my son would not turn out like his mom.

But how was I going to prevent that from happening?

I decided to take some classes in childhood development and loved it. The knowledge and the skills I gained were exactly what I needed to raise a happy, healthy human who could face any challenge with more resilience and character than had been developed in me. I accepted help from mentors, therapists, and community services that loved me through some very tough times.

In the mid-1990s, The Centers for Disease Control and Kaiser Permanente did a study on how adverse childhood experiences (ACEs) may negatively affect adult health. ACEs include childhood abuse, living with a family member in distress, growing up with substance abuse in the immediate family system, experiencing neglect, and more. The troubling data showed how these traumas often develop young adults who become addicts, go to jail, or become mentally or physically sick, and even experience an early death. However, some of the children with high ACE scores don't. It turned out that every one of those children had at least one adult in their life who decided to invest in them. They found love and guidance from at least one caring individual and, with their help, developed the grit needed to overcome the hard life challenges.

When I saw this research, I understood why my three sons turned into three men who are secure, capable, and achieving their dreams with partners who love and respect their character and strong principles. They are unique and so completely themselves as well as committed to helping others, despite what they faced in their childhood.

You see, as they were growing up, I was using all of my newfound knowledge with them while also navigating an adulthood more like the one that unfolds for most children with high ACE scores. In the first two decades of their lives, they had a mother who loved them dearly and also suffered with depression, medical conditions managed by prescriptions, and mental abuse that led to divorce. It wasn't easy for any of us.

It wasn't until my youngest was four years old that I finally began to apply my Teach Joy philosophy to restore my own personal well-being and showed my sons what a strong woman looked and acted like.

But the kids. They are okay. No, they are way better than okay. They are phenomenal. Why? Because they had one human, albeit imperfect and navigating a bunch of disasters, who made sure all their needs were met and gave them an environment in which they could learn self-love, autonomy, and compassion. They had one human who created experiences in which they could develop all their skills and who, most importantly, provided unconditional love. Someone who, despite her own challenges, modeled a passion for life and a strong desire to make the world a better place. And because of that one person, they thrived and continue to thrive today.

The same can be true for your children.

WHAT YOUR CHILD REALLY NEEDS

Your children don't need a perfect parent with a perfect life. They don't need you to run yourself ragged with endless lists of to-dos and to-bes. They need you to be in a relationship with them, to love each moment of learning together with patience and grace. They need to see the emotions you have and how you solve problems and confront challenges. They need honesty and intention and to be spoken to with encouragement, kindness, and respect so they will treat others well. They need fun and silly moments to be able to be a kid, and they need experiences that will inspire them to fall in love with learning and become lifelong-learners.

They need an adult who knows how to cultivate their social, emotional, cognitive, creative, and physical needs, so that they will have the resilience they need to face life's inevitable challenges. They need to be able to feel confident in their own abilities and opinions. The goal is for your kiddos to collect a toolbox full of techniques to get through their own life challenges as they grow into adulthood.

That's exactly why I've put this instruction manual together for you.

This is the resource I wished I had when I was a teenage mom and determined to do better by my child, and I've done my best to make it a simple resource for you to use in every phase of your child's development through their first five years.

But hey, applying the philosophy to children older than five (and maybe even adults) is going to give you incredible results as well.

THE POWER OF TEACHING JOY

In May 2016, I developed a non-profit learning center around my teaching philosophy. The name is the focus of the program—Training Educating And Mentoring Services—doing business as TEAMS Learning Center. These child development centers offer hands-on, play-based education for young children as well as the adults who love and care for them.

Training parents and new teachers, interns, and student teachers was my first attempt to transform Early Childhood Education, which is quite possibly one of the most under-resourced and unappreciated professional sectors. As parents learned how to nurture their children's branches during Stay-and-Plays and everyone began to see the results of this approach, a beautiful community formed around these children to find more resources.

In seven years, we served more than 3,000 children, many of whom faced learning challenges and would not have been ready, let alone thrived, in kindergarten if not for our intentional and playful interventions. The community is so thrilled about the work we are doing that they awarded us the 2023 Non-profit of the Year award. (For more information, scan this QR code.)

My personal dream is to make this philosophy and standard of excellence the status quo across the nation, and this book is my first step to inviting parents, educators, and change-makers like you to join me in that effort.

And it starts with you and your child.

HOW TO USE THIS BOOK TO NURTURE YOUR CHILD

There are five core areas of development that your child has that need to be understood, nurtured, challenged, practiced, and celebrated. As soon as you begin reading this book, you'll understand why we call them branches of development.

The truth is, we only have a small amount of time in life, when our child is learning and growing at such a rapid pace, to develop these areas.

Socially, we need to help them learn from and connect with others. Emotionally, we want to help them feel secure, confident, and capable. Cognitively, we can help them be able to comprehend and execute directions. Creatively, we can cultivate their ability to express themselves and their ideas and opinions. Physically, we want them to be healthy inside and out with self-help skills, so they can be independent.

This book is designed to help you understand what's happening in your child's body, mind, heart, and soul in each phase, and then equip you with some activities, books, and even songs that will help you nurture each developmental branch of their growing self. On the left pages, you will find a story to inspire your children. On the right, you will find all the information you will need to begin nurturing that phase in your child.

In fact, I suggest you approach this book in the following manner.

1. Pull your little one onto your lap and read the children's story to them. Leave all the adult information out, of course.
2. When your child is playing or sleeping, open this book again. This time, go to the page where Joy is the same age as your child. If your child is just turning one, go to the page where Joy is doing the same.
3. Read through the information I've placed on the pages facing Joy's story during that phase. Discover what your child is experiencing in that phase socially, emotionally, cognitively, creatively, and physically. Check out all the activities, books, and songs that will help you nurture their development.
4. Then, spend a few minutes creating a little plan for your next day that includes these activities and tools.
5. After each day's play, I suggest writing down what your child really seemed to love and even where they struggled. This type of journaling will help you keep track of your child's skill-building, identify areas in which you can create more support, and celebrate every milestone.

When you spend intentional time with your child and understand their interests, and focus on supporting the phase they are in, you are giving them the essentials to not only thrive but contribute to the betterment of our world.

If you're ready to learn about what's happening naturally in your child's mind, body, heart, and soul, and what you can do to nurture all of it toward health and joy, let's get started!

This is Joy.
She is new to the world and already learning.
New branches form and strengthen
with each interaction and experience.

DEVELOPMENTAL AREA WITHIN A SPECIFIC AGE

In these sections, you will find a simple definition of the area of development being focused on—social, emotional, cognitive, creative, or physical—and how it relates to that age. The first year, it is essential to do your best because 80% of a person's development happens the first year and 90% is complete by the age of 6. This time is so very important, and I hope you will use this book as a guide to have fun while you do your best to bring the hands-on learning into your child's everyday experience that nurtures every part of them as they grow up.

ACTIVITIES AND EXAMPLES

In these sections, there are suggestions for fun, interactive activities you can do with your little ones. You will find ways to enhance the development during this specific time of growth. The more engaged you are, the more your child will be. Enthusiasm is caught, not taught, so play with a purpose and remember to have fun!

KEY POINT

In these sections, you will discover a key area to focus on and important topics to understand as well as little nuggets of wisdom to help you enjoy this phase.

Whether you are their parent, auntie, or daycare provider, you can adapt and apply these based on your role.

These early years are when you are investing in a child's future success. It's important to appreciate how precious this time is and know that they are always watching and learning from what you are doing. Make sure you are showing them skills that will help them develop healthy habits for their future.

Enjoy your time and have fun. If children are having fun, they are engaged in learning.

TEACHER JOY'S BOOKSHELF

I've included some of my favorite books to read to young children.

Check out your local library, search online for videos of these books being read aloud, or purchase these books to read and share with more children. These are always great gift ideas too. The gift of a good book lasts a lifetime.

TEACHER JOY'S SONGBOOK

Singing songs to young children helps them in so many ways. You should know that they don't care if you sing well or not. They just like hearing you sing. Scan this QR code to go directly to *Teacher Joy's Songbook* to hear how the songs are sung.

Meeting her family for the first time and getting to know those around her nurtures her SOCIAL branch.

SOCIAL DEVELOPMENT AND NEWBORNS

Social development is about developing relationships with others. The relationship can be with a parent, a pet, a sibling, a friend, a grandparent, or a stranger. The WHO is not the point. It is the experience of meeting and forming a relationship that is the absolute goal. Socialization includes communication, expression, eye contact, and more. It's important to interact with the motive of connecting and engaging with their soul to really get to know them. Enjoy observing them with the intention of continuing to gain an understanding of who they are. The social branch thrives with love and attention but can be damaged by neglect.

SOCIAL ACTIVITIES AND EXAMPLES

Newborn babies sleep, eat, poop and cry. However, there are moments of alertness that give you a chance to engage in socialization. During the first months of welcoming a new baby into your class, home, or life, remember that everything is brand new and should be introduced to them. Bring objects and people into their line of sight, up close, and allow a long period of time for focusing and exploration with all of their senses.

Play the repeat game. Every sound the baby makes, repeat the same sound back to them.

Position a mirror in front of them, so they can see themselves and watch their expressions.

Sing songs to babies. Sing lullabies when you want to calm them down, using your voice and tone to sooth them to sleep or just more ease. Sing fun and silly songs while they are awake and hum when you are not sure what to sing. See TEACHER JOY'S SONGBOOK below for ideas.

THE FIRST LOVE IS THE STRONGEST

Socialization begins long before babies are born. They can hear and sense the people who are around most often, forming bonds before ever meeting, so make sure to love on that belly.

Birth is a traumatic experience for babies, even with the easiest labor and delivery. They are entering a whole new and very overwhelming world, so all they need those first few days and weeks is calm love.

Share the love of your little love. It is so important to allow others to have one-on-one time with your baby. Forming bonds and relationships create trust and can help with separation anxiety in later months and years.

TEACHER JOY'S BOOKSHELF

Baby Faces by Margret Miller is full of diverse facial expressions.

Guess How Much I Love You by Sam McBratney is a sweet story showing a parent's love.

TEACHER JOY'S SONGBOOK

BYE BABY BUNTING

Refer to a different person in the child's life each time you repeat this song. Introduce friends and family members that live far away or a loved one who has passed away. It can last as long as you need it to, as sometimes it takes many, many verses to calm a baby down. Set the intention for the energy as you sing. When they are loud and fussy, start fast and then slow down gradually, and they will calm with your energy as you engage a lower, more monotone voice.

Feeling welcomed and loved,
baby Joy grows her
EMOTIONAL branch.

EMOTIONAL DEVELOPMENT AND NEWBORNS

Emotional development, simply explained, happens in the feelings part of the brain. Really stop and think for a moment of all the different emotions one experiences in a day. They all started as a newborn. Babies are born with the basic vocal tools and they learn how to use them through experiences and practice. They learn in time to say how they feel, but in the beginning, they are exploring and discovering the power of their voice. Try not to react with frustration when it's upsetting. Instead, accept how they feel, label their emotion, speak calmly, and problem-solve out loud what you can do with them to make them feel better.

EMOTIONAL ACTIVITIES AND EXAMPLES

Try out different variations in your voice, sing, hum, talk deep, or act surprised. When you show how you feel and own emotions, you are modeling what they don't yet know they are capable of.

Read storybooks every day. Get new books often and really make the characters come to life with different voices and accents. Have some fun exposing your newborn to sounds.

Read children's picture books with real baby faces and act out each emotion you read. Let your baby see the book up close for a long time to see the image and then your face too.

Avoid extremely loud noises or abrupt movements. The birthing process was hard enough.

PAYING ATTENTION PAYS OFF

If you listen closely enough, a baby will tell you their needs with the tone of their cry. To gain that knowledge, you have to allow them to cry and then pay close attention, watch their body language, and listen to their pitch and tone.

In the beginning, it is not about teaching them our language. It is about learning theirs.

Follow the natural flow of their daily schedule of eating, sleeping, and diapering needs.

It helps set you up for success.

Record your observations and chart the daily routine, so you will be able to prepare what you need before the baby tells you.

Avoid long periods of stress in a newborn and offer reassurance with your voice and hugs.

TEACHER JOY'S BOOKSHELF

I Like Myself by Karen Beaumont is a wonderful self-empowering book, and the *What Do You Do With An Idea* series by Kobi Yamada creates inspiring and awesome story time.

TEACHER JOY'S SONGBOOK

I'VE BEEN WAITING FOR YOU TO COME TO THIS PLACE by Bev Boss

Repeat this song until you achieve your goal. It can be used to gather children or transition from one space to another without everyone going at once, as a welcoming song, or to discover likes and dislikes. It can also teach vocabulary for foods, activities, or a specific subject. Above all, it teaches children to love everyone, regardless of their preferences.

As she becomes aware of her surroundings, Joy's mind is starting to form its COGNITIVE branch.

COGNITIVE DEVELOPMENT AND NEWBORNS

This is the thinking part of the brain, where they take in, analyze, and store information and form the knowledge of what things are and how they work. This skill that is so valuable in this ever-changing world that needs strong, problem-solving minds, starts at birth. The mind is rapidly trying to learn at incredible speeds during the developmental years. Value and cherish these moments and enjoy solving problems together.

COGNITIVE ACTIVITIES AND EXAMPLES

Introduce objects like rattles, wooden spoons, metal bowls, wicker baskets, safe household items, or objects outside in nature and tell baby all about them. This gives them exposure to language as well as the opportunity to see and learn new things and feel new textures.

Wind chimes and musical instruments are great to introduce new sounds early on.

You really cannot talk too much. Use a large variety of words to strengthen language.

Protect newborn babies from overwhelming noises, busy places, and harmful air. The very young are so fragile and defenseless, they need our direct protection and care.

MILESTONES OF PROGRESS

Every child develops differently, but there are some general guidelines that let us know if a child is not progressing as they should. If we can identify areas of delay early on, we can add support where it is needed. It is valuable to have an awareness of what your baby should be able to do and around when.

What to Expect The First Year by Heidi Murkoff is a simple reference guide.

There are also many online tools for tracking developmental milestones. Your pediatrician may have a good recommendation as well.

I have learned incredible amounts from other moms, too, about what to expect next and how to solve the little unexpected challenges. Build friendships with parents and ask for advice from caregivers and grandparents.

TEACHER JOY'S BOOKSHELF

Counting Kisses by Karen Katz is a sweet book promoting counting, affection, and interaction.

Caps for Sale by Esphyr Slobodkina is a perfect book for every age child and adult.

TEACHER JOY'S SONGBOOK

THE BEAR WENT OVER THE MOUNTAIN

Sit on the ground, hold baby on your knees, and move with the words.

This is a modification of an old classic that teaches words that describe actions and provides an opportunity for fun, interactive movement to engage physical muscles. It can also be used to ask kids about what they see or even something they imagine. Later it can be used as a traveling game, like an "I Spy," by ending with, "And what do you see?"

Joy starts to express herself by making noises and begins to grow her CREATIVE branch.

CREATIVE DEVELOPMENT AND NEWBORNS

One's creativity begins upon arrival. This area of their being is made up of their own unique self-expression, responses to the environment, and their opinions as they form them. Each child should be celebrated for what they personally bring to this world. It is up to us to discover who they are, with their natural talents and interests. As we learn who they are, we can enhance their capabilities by giving them intentional skills to practice as they develop their imagination and creativity. This development is best done through engaging them in play.

CREATIVE ACTIVITIES AND EXAMPLES

Have fun with your pitch and tone. When you talk, use a deep voice, sing, whisper or grunt. Just have a good time and make fun sounds and create made-up noises.

Fill their life with creative people. Model expression in every form, from music to colors in their environment to different textures, and rotate new toys to keep things fun and fresh.

Hold baby within a foot of your face and make funny facial expressions repeatedly and see if they will mimic your movements. Jean Claude Piaget was the philosophist who first modeled how infants only hours old can learn and mimic sticking their tongues out.

Appreciate this moment and every facial expression, coo, and movement.

EXPRESS YOUR CREATIVITY

What fun it can be to be a new parent, grandparent, or family member. Newborns are perfectly precious and so easy to fall in love with. Enjoy showing your natural expressions of love and welcome as they arrive.

Get in touch with your silly side and enjoy being childlike. We all deserve a break from reality and grown-up thinking to enjoy the moment.

If you can't find your silly side, pretend that you can. If it helps, try loosening up by dancing to a silly song or reading a fun book. Dr. Seuss always seems to tickle my funny bone. Try *Green Eggs and Ham* or another fun rhyming book. I can't seem to get through *The Wonky Donkey* by Craig Smith without cracking up myself.

TEACHER JOY'S BOOKSHELF

Today I Feel Silly by Jamie Lee Curtis and *My Many Colored Days* by Dr. Seuss teach us how to be silly as we go through the emotions, teaching colors and feelings, using vibrant illustrations.

TEACHER JOY'S SONGBOOK

LITTLE PETER RABBIT

Each time you repeat this song, refer to (and touch) a different body part as you mention it.

In addition to teaching body parts, it increases fine motor control and use of their pointer finger as they grow. It can last as long as you want, while you stall to wait for something or transition a group of littles from one place to another. Make it more fun and involve the older kiddos by asking them to pick the body part.

Baby Joy moves her body and
feels the wind as it blows,
creating her PHYSICAL branch.

PHYSICAL DEVELOPMENT AND NEWBORNS

Physical development is how the body grows, inside and out. A newborn can move all their parts but not in a controlled way. That will take practice and time as well as interest. Keep encouraging and providing chances for different physical movements. Use caregiving times, like diapering or bath time, to use soft physical touch to support their developmental growth. Provide a safe space for them to lay down on their back and on their belly with direct supervision. Sometimes it helps to get down on your belly face-to-face for an interactive tummy-time.

PHYSICAL ACTIVITIES AND EXAMPLES

Give newborn babies the opportunity to wiggle about without restrictions, as well as time for snuggling up close and swaddling up snug as a bug in a rug.

Infant massage is a great way to engage baby in gentle movement and calm their body with an introduction to tactile and sensory awareness.

As long as it is not too hot or too cold, bring the baby out a few moments to feel the natural elements each day. Fresh air and sunshine are healthy.

A warm washcloth wipe down or a soothing bath with Mom or Dad can feel good to their bodies as well as calm agitation. It's important that they feel that physical connection and touch.

THE IMPORTANCE OF SELF-CARE

Model healthy habits such as walking and exercising and eating healthy foods. If you are a nursing mom, make good choices about what you are eating to give your baby the healthiest start.

Postpartum depression is very real and there are two suggestions I have for you to prevent or conquer your depression. Number one, walk outside anytime you feel down. The endorphins from walking and breathing fresh air have magical healing properties. The second is to find a friend. Being alone and isolating may feel more comfortable in the moment, but it makes it harder in the long run. So get up, call a friend, and build your personal support system. If you are a loved one in the life of the mama, reach out regularly.

TEACHER JOY'S BOOKSHELF

Silly Sally by Audrey Wood, *Head to Toe* by Eric Carle, and *I Am Enough* by Grace Byers are interactive stories about body movements that are also fun to read.

TEACHER JOY'S SONGBOOK

TOE-KNEE-CHEST-NUT

Touch the body part as you say it.
Knock on your head when you say NUT.
Cross your chest when you say LOVE.

Start slow and each time you sing it, speed up until you just can't sing any faster. It's a good way to get kiddos to move and bend. Combine it with morning stretches and/or use it to transition to high-energy movements.

As Joy grows, she learns more and more. She meets more family and neighbors and her SOCIAL branches stretch and grow. During her first year, she makes her first friend, Bo the dog.

SOCIAL DEVELOPMENT AND THE FIRST YEAR

Connection is the key to social success in life. Why not give our children the gift of confidence and self-worth? This first year is the foundation that every single relationship will build upon for the rest of that sweet little baby's life, and we have the power to fill their environment with positive, safe, and nurturing people all of the time. Treat every moment with great care and purpose. This is the investment in their future, and it comes in the form of your time and attention, making sure they have a happy and fulfilling learning environment wherever they are and at all times.

SOCIAL ACTIVITIES AND EXAMPLES

Role-play with stuffed animals or dolls in front of your baby, making up regular everyday conversations about life and daily happenings with different voices.

Bring them around other babies and let them watch each other. Provide a rich but not overwhelming social environment. Too many children is not ideal.

Pets are such a great addition to a baby's life. Model kindness and redirect baby from hard touches with a loving voice and clear boundaries, "Oh no. Gentle touches with kitty."

Talk about familiar people when they are gone so they gain recognition.

THEY ARE ALWAYS WATCHING!

A baby's brain is working so hard every day, collecting what they see, hear, and feel. What they soak in forms who they become. Make sure their space is full of love, laughter, and respect rather than stress, abuse, and fear. Protect babies from negative emotions and experiences.

The television, the music you listen to, the conversations you have in front of them—these are the things you can control.

When you talk in front of them, say nice things about them. If you are complaining all of the time about not getting any sleep, they feel, see, and hear those comments.

Give them opportunities to watch in nature, on outings, happy relationships and fun with friends. Show them how you want them to love their partner when they are grown.

TEACHER JOY'S BOOKSHELF

Whoever You Are by Mem Fox and *My Papi Has a Motorcycle* by Isabel Quintero are simple books teaching diversity and love for one another.

TEACHER JOY'S SONGBOOK

YOU ARE MY SUNSHINE

Repeat until your child falls asleep or dramatize your emotions while singing.

You can start fast and super expressive and end as a soft lullaby to calm or aid in sleep, or you can sing to give the experience of the dramatic change in tone from happy to sad. Then as you sing, start to slow the dramatic emotion to a calm, mundane tone.

Sometimes it's scary to meet new people or go to new places, but Joy always feels happy when her puppy is around. She is growing EMOTIONALLY every time she feels new feelings.

EMOTIONAL DEVELOPMENT AND THE FIRST YEAR

No one baby is just like another. Each individual is creating their own character. They take what their parents gave them through their genes and physical being, and then they use their surroundings and exposure to new things to fill in the remainder. This first year of emotional development will make all of the difference in their executive function (worth looking up) if you support them in not just solving their immediate needs, but by walking them through how to get their needs met. When they are crying, use different methods than feeding or picking them up and rocking them. Try reassuring them by talking or singing, distracting them with an object or a game.

EMOTIONAL ACTIVITIES AND EXAMPLES

Play Peek-A-Boo to practice emotions: surprise, anticipation, object permanence, and glee.

Water play is such a fun-filled yet soothing activity. Bath time is always a good idea, even if they are not dirty and even if it is not a bathtub. Water has healing powers.

There is something special about a swing or a sway that calms us down. Create an opportunity to swing at a park, at home, or just with your body when it helps.

Bubbles are a must for generating fun. Make your own homemade bubble solution by combining dish soap, warm water, and a small dab of liquid glycerin. Play until perfect.

SELF-SOOTHING PRACTICE AND CALMING TECHNIQUES

Use your emotions to calm their emotions. Take deep breaths, count slowly, visualize calm and happy feelings, and say affirmations out loud. You are not just helping you and baby in the moment; you are modeling what they need to do to self-soothe.

Provide tools like a lovie, a binkie, or a blanket, and let your baby find what makes them feel better. If you are quick to solve their every need, or if they only fall asleep by eating, then they are not getting a chance to practice valuable skills at this important time.

It's okay for babies to feel frustrated because they gain such a grand sense of fulfillment when they are able to figure it out.

TEACHER JOY'S BOOKSHELF

Watch out, friends, the book *Love You Forever* by Robert Munsch is an adult tear-jerker!

Oh, The Places You'll Go by Dr. Seuss is my personal all-time favorite book.

TEACHER JOY'S SONGBOOK

IF YOU'RE HAPPY AND YOU KNOW IT

Repeat, each time doing a different action. Example: Stomp your feet, act out and identify different emotions, get creative and add some fun ones in as you sing the verses. Another fun option with older kiddos is to keep stacking the movements onto the end with every repetition. You can also have kiddos act out the emotion while others guess and mimic the actions.

The first year of learning is full of trying out new things, and Joy's COGNITIVE skills are growing each time she eats, moves, or watches the world and the people around her.

COGNITIVE DEVELOPMENT AND THE FIRST YEAR

A baby needs to be able to explore and discover their world and be safe to do so. If a child always has boundaries and the word "no" said to them often, they will learn to not try or develop fear around new experiences. This is the time for them to see how things work. If the only toys they have are plastic that make sounds when they touch them, then they are only learning one skill—instant gratification. Diversify the toys they play with and rotate new ones in to master new skills and abilities.

COGNITIVE ACTIVITIES AND EXAMPLES

Open-ended explorations invite the baby to do whatever they want with what they are exploring. They will put it in their mouth, hit it against things, and inspect it. Make sure you give them a variety of objects and textures that are safe and supervised without boundaries. Please, mamas, do not give them your keys and cell phones.

Hide and seek small objects. Get their interest and then cover it, so baby will have to look for it.

Cause and effect is a cool game. Try knocking a block tower down, or dump and fill bowls, shovels in the sandbox, or cups in the bath. Making sensory bottles are great ways to learn.

LET'S TALK ABOUT TALKING!

Long before they are learning to speak themselves, they are learning to talk by listening. Be clear and slow. Repeat what you are saying. Say it in different ways and in sign language too. You simply cannot talk too much to babies!

When they jibber-jabber, this is their way of pre-talking. Act as if you understand them and respond in conversation.

Language is such a vital skill in every person's life. If you are blessed enough to be bilingual, please influence your baby's life with the beautiful gift of language.

Explain everything you are doing, what you see, and what your plan is for the day. Describe the world around you and how things work. Never stop talking!

Research the 30-million-word gap.

It will blow your mind!!!

TEACHER JOY'S BOOKSHELF

The Very Hungry Caterpillar by Eric Carle and *Pete the Cat* books, and *I Love My White Shoes* and *His Four Groovy Buttons* by Eric Litwin are fun read-aloud books.

TEACHER JOY'S SONGBOOK

THIS IS NUMBER 1

Hide your hands behind your back and bring them out one at a time, showing the number of fingers, and roll hands around each other. Then hold up the number of fingers at the end. Continue until you get to 5 fingers. Stop there or go back down to 1.

Introduce and practice numbers and fine motor control, observation of counting fingers, or sign language for numbers counting to 10. Or simplify to count to 5 as attention allows, using movement to engage again. You can also use this song to teach numbers in another language.

As each new way to express herself comes to life, so does her CREATIVITY. She uses her voice to get her needs met, coos and smiles, and makes so much noise by banging things together.

CREATIVE DEVELOPMENT AND THE FIRST YEAR

The time you spend building creativity while they are still babies is something that they will benefit from forevermore. Fill their world with variety. Different music to hear, things to see, and objects to safely explore are the minimum. You can also enhance this area of development by introducing child-friendly paint to make art creations or provide musical instruments and show them how music is made. Drums and xylophones make fun sounds. Expose them to art of every medium and expression.

CREATIVE ACTIVITIES AND EXAMPLES

Embrace the silly. Laugh often and completely. Babies are funny and when they know you are laughing at them, they will do things to make you laugh. Encourage this!

Baby-safe paint can be made by mixing food coloring with salt, flour, and water. Still discourage them from putting it in their mouth to prevent bad habits.

Place their toys on a low shelf for them to be able to access and explore independently.

Introduce loose-part toys such as blocks, cars, stacking bowls, balls, and animal toys to create open-ended play opportunities.

MAKING DECISIONS FOR THE FUTURE

Being a decisive person starts by being given the options to choose what you want when you are a baby. Why not give them two toys or spoons for eating to choose from? Present them with their options and give them time to reach out for the one they want.

This is the beginning of forming their opinions. Give limited options, so as not to overwhelm them and pose the question to them, "Which one would you like?"

The art of listening to their opinion builds confidence as they grow. This method also provides an opportunity for pre-talking instead of crying or whining to get what they want. If you give them the words and model how to say the answers, this is a habit that will pay off as they start to form real words to express their wants and needs.

TEACHER JOY'S BOOKSHELF

The Wide-Mouthed Frog by Keith Faulkner and *If You Give a Mouse a Cookie* by Laura Numeroff (and other books in her series) give a perfect opportunity to change your voice to fit the characters and really use your facial expressions to bring the story to life.

TEACHER JOY'S SONGBOOK

PUT A WAVE IN YOUR HANDS

Act out the motions as you sing, changing the motion and body part each time you repeat.

Examples: Clap your hands, stomp your feet, slap your knee, etc.

Use this fun, welcoming song to say hello or to teach the vocabulary of body parts and movements. You can also use this as a circle time song with a group of kids to introduce each kiddo. With older children, a good option is to have them choose the actions.

COGNITIVE
CREATIVE
EMOTIONAL
PHYSICAL
SOCIAL
As the first year moves along, so does Joy's growth. She gets bigger and bigger. As she moves, she figures out the different parts she has and how they work. Her PHYSICAL branches are growing fast.

PHYSICAL DEVELOPMENT AND THE FIRST YEAR

What a significant year for physical growth and mastering their body's movements. In the beginning of their first year, you will see how much effort they give to grasping something to get it in their mouth to explore it. Then as the year moves on, you can watch how they are able to roll over, scoot, crawl, sit up, cruise, feed themselves, and maybe even walk without assistance. This year is huge in their physical development. Watch for them to hit all of those major milestones and celebrate each one.

PHYSICAL ACTIVITIES AND EXAMPLES

Provide a safe and comfortable space with freedom to move for tummy-time in the beginning. Then allow for safe rolling space, and move furniture out of the way to create open areas.

Put toys just out of reach for them to strive, making them want to move toward it.

As they start to master crawling, set up obstacles like pillows or cushions to crawl over.

Fine motor skills are built by giving them things they can do with their fingertips—pulling grass; playing with tags on the edge of a blanket, beans inside of a sealed bag, and buttons sewn on fabric; finger-painting; using markers; picking up small non-choking items.

HEALTHY FOOD HABITS START EARLY

In the beginning, there is breast milk, specially-designed to be the best food for baby. What Mom eats while nursing should be the best nutrition-rich foods possible. Formula is an alternative, and you may have to try different ones to find your baby's right fit. Baby's body language will show you when they have a burp.

Between 4-6 months, introduce baby food. Start with single-ingredient infant cereal thinned to soup consistency and thicken as time goes on. Introduce vegetables, then fruits, the same way. Start with one at a time for a few days to allow baby's body to learn to digest the new food. Whole healthy foods are always best.

When they can sit without support, begin to introduce safe self-feeding foods like banana chunks, peas, or cereal for them to work on their finger muscles.

TEACHER JOY'S BOOKSHELF

Piggies by Audrey and Don Wood has fantastic illustrations to show the realism of fingers and the imagination of piggies. *Planting a Rainbow* by Lois Ehlert shows healthy food being raised in the garden.

TEACHER JOY'S SONGBOOK

RAM SAM SAM

Engage body movements with this silly, repeated-action song. Build on movements each time, slow to fast, loud to quiet, or just the movements with no sound at all.

You can change the words to put 3 different objects together to create a different story too, using the same syllable-beat and tone.

Joy celebrates her first birthday and so many friends and family come to see her. Everyone makes such funny faces when they arrive. Now her SOCIAL branch grows and stretches to those close by.

SOCIAL DEVELOPMENT AND ONE-YEAR-OLDS

Toddlers love other toddlers, though they have yet to develop the understanding of each other's feelings. The way to learn is to practice. They are still in an ego-centric state of mind in which they are the center of their world. All of the food, people, and experiences are just for them. They spend their time mastering newly-developed skills and testing their boundaries socially. Give them a challenging environment to keep them learning and interested in developing these social skills. Observe other children and people with them, explain what you see, and provide a rich social experience during this time.

SOCIAL ACTIVITIES AND EXAMPLES

Jumping on a cushion placed on the ground instead of jumping off the couch, or kicking a ball instead of a pet, or hitting a pillow instead of a person are ways to teach them redirection.

Mimicking how we play, talk, or move is how babies learn. Get down on their level and play with your toddler, using puzzles, connecting toys, and blocks.

What a great time to expose them to different cultures, languages, and diversity. Use books, pictures, videos, and people in your community to show them differences.

Role-play with play people. Use figures showing different sizes, colors, and physical abilities.

SUCCESSFUL REDIRECTION

They want to see the reaction to their actions. This is the time to teach them boundaries and engage them through redirection. When they do or touch something unsafe or unkind, replace it with a better option or distract them with a healthy outlet for their desired skill.

Sharing their things is especially hard for this age group. If you have several children, make sure there are multiple toys of the same kind, so each child can have their own.

Communicate in simple-to-understand, repetitive words, using clear language. Use the tone of your voice to get their attention, verbally set boundaries, and then engage them in building the skills they are showing an interest in and have fun doing right things with them.

TEACHER JOY'S BOOKSHELF

The Relatives Came by Cynthia Rylant, *Are You My Mother* by P.D. Eastman, and *Happy Birthday Moon* by Frank Asch are fun books to read.

TEACHER JOY'S SONGBOOK

MAY THERE ALWAYS BE SUNSHINE

Start your circle time or activity with this song to let the students know that it is time to begin. This allows a clear separation between social time and listening time.

A fun way to mix it up is to change the third line in the song to teach a new sign and empower the kids to share who is important to them. It's also great for teaching sign language.

Joy is growing in her emotions and gets frustrated when she cannot do something or get somewhere. Each day she gets excited to go outside, she is practicing new EMOTIONAL skills.

EMOTIONAL DEVELOPMENT AND ONE-YEAR-OLDS

This is the time when they are starting to experience fear with stranger danger, separation anxiety, and getting hurt. It's not just loud noises or being left alone anymore. Their awareness is increasing and opening their world up a little more with each passing day. They are also taking more time to notice the little things like insects crawling on the ground or tiny things they want to explore by putting them in their mouth. This is a time when you need to be very aware of what they are doing with close supervision, yet not hover or interfere with their discoveries. Just be available to remove something unsafe.

EMOTIONAL ACTIVITIES AND EXAMPLES

When frustration sets in, teach them to shake it off or take a deep breath and to try again.

Wooden blocks are one of the most successful tools to teach overcoming frustration. They get to practice balancing and dexterity, and then the blocks fall, and they get to try again.

Balloons, balls, and bubbles always bring excitement and sometimes other emotions too.

Introduce child-safe playdough. (Homemade is best.) It provides sensory resistance and really allows for soft or hard play to happen.

BUILDING CONFIDENCE AND TEACHING SELF-REGULATION

You are building their confidence like you build a house, brick by brick, only it's more like tear by tear. Start with a plan. Have patience with the process. Stay positive, encouraging, and understanding as they learn through trial and error. Provide the tools to be successful like baby gates for safety, teaching toys for engagement, and love and attention for reassurance, and you will be impressed with how your baby grows.

Age appropriate activities means mixing skills they can easily master in addition to things just outside of their skill set. Save the 20-piece puzzle or tiny Legos for later. Start with bigger, easier to connect toys to build their ability and confidence at the same time.

TEACHER JOY'S BOOKSHELF

Go Away Big Green Monster by Ed Emberley and *We're Going on a Bear Hunt* by Michael Rosen are great books to overcome fears.

TEACHER JOY'S SONGBOOK

KOOKABURRA

Practice silly tones and great emotional expressions with this song. It also has a good rhythm to teach singing verses and building a whole story as the song continues.

Add the challenge to sing in a round. An example of this approach can be found online at We Play Along—Kookaburra on YouTube.

Everything in Joy's world is new, and each new experience is a new learning opportunity. Seeing what happens next is her favorite game, like what happens when her water spills on Bo. Her COGNITIVE branch is growing wild because her curiosity keeps her thinking.

COGNITIVE DEVELOPMENT AND ONE-YEAR-OLDS

Playing starts to become fun and more interactive at this age. They are paying attention to what you are doing and interested in exploring beyond playing with the object you give them. They want more outside their reach. Foster this curiosity by expanding their world and its contents. Bring more interesting foods and experiences for your toddler to expand their knowledge base. Don't be too quick to react. Instead provide the space for exploration, set yourself up for success, and do messy projects outside with extra towels.

COGNITIVE ACTIVITIES AND EXAMPLES

Simple manipulatives to connect, build, and create with (pop beads, Mega blocks, knob or chunky puzzles, magnetic tiles, linking chains, bigger piece, toddler-friendly toys) are great for this phase.

Books, books, and more books! Provide your toddler with board books. Teach them respect for literature by putting paper books up and not letting them rip pages or color on them.

Sign language or baby sign is a magnificent, empowering tool to improve communication and learn what they want.

ENGAGING A CHILD INTO PLAY

I use the concept of engaging throughout this book, as it is a crucial part to the success of teaching through play. This means getting down on their level and playing and modeling how to do the activity with excitement. Enthusiasm is caught, not taught. If you are engaged, it will trigger their interest as well.

Don't expect your toddler to master independent play just yet. They need your involvement in addition to time to practice by themselves to gain the skill.

While playing with your toddler, you should talk about what you are doing and add in the experience of describing words such as colors, shapes, and textures to influence their language development.

Follow their interests and keep introducing new options.

TEACHER JOY'S BOOKSHELF

Rosie's Walk by Pat Hutchins offers great visuals showing cause and good use of positional words like under, over, through, and around. *One Bean* by Anne Rockwell shows growth, and *Jump Frog Jump* by Robert Kalan is good for speaking with repetition.

TEACHER JOY'S SONGBOOK

5 GREEN AND SPECKLED FROGS

This countdown song about frogs jumping into a pool can be a great transition or waiting song. Each frog that jumps in catches a different kind of bug for an interactive teachable moment.

It's also fun to make a flannel board or create a hands-on craft opportunity to play as they sing.

Eating is so much fun. Joy is finding what she likes and doesn't, forming her own opinion about food. She squeals in delight when she finds things funny like Bo licking her.

CREATIVE DEVELOPMENT AND ONE-YEAR-OLDS

This is when things start to get really fun. Older siblings even want to play with the baby now because they can do more and engage for longer and they don't feel as fragile. They are getting the hang of those physical skills, and that gives them the freedom to discover further and expand their own opinions and interests. Sing the songs and fingerplays. Watch videos online to learn and then teach your toddler live in person. Ask other friends and family to teach you both songs they know too. Singing is a great way to pass time in the car or as you are cooking to keep their attention as well as foster their creative voices. Enjoy how easy they are to redirect. Catch their attention or distract as needed.

CREATIVE ACTIVITIES AND EXAMPLES

Let them play with their food, as they are learning. Plus, kids are 100% washable.

You will need to consistently redirect them to draw on the paper and not in their mouths, but yes, give them markers, crayons, chalk, pencils, paint pens, colored pencils, and pens.

The little toddler booty shake is truly one of the best gifts in life. Turn music on and encourage dancing to the beat. You will have to practice your own dance moves too.

Add dramatic play to their environment with hats and scarves. Simple to get on and fun to wear.

Pretend food and real pots and pans or their own Tupperware drawer in the kitchen are great tools to aid in their creative role-playing. They will mimic the life they see around them.

WATCH WHAT THEY ARE WATCHING

I have been a student of toddlers for about 30 years, and they have taught me so much! If you can really follow their interests, you will find out what their natural talents are in the very beginning of their life. Give them more of what they want, as well as supporting the skills in areas they need, so they can grow to their highest potential. The best sports stars were most definitely given balls to play with when they were young, and engineers clearly loved the assembly of toys and what makes them work.

Filtering the influence of media is so vital, as advertisers are trying to attract them to want what they are selling. This diminishes their natural interests and replaces it with whatever is trending.

TEACHER JOY'S BOOKSHELF

Where The Wild Things Are by Maurice Sendak and *Goodnight Moon* by Margaret Wise Brown are fantastic picture books. *The Night Gardener* by the Fan Brothers offers great pictures of creativity and curiosity.

TEACHER JOY'S SONGBOOK

MR. CLOWN

Practice taking turns, expand creative expression, connect body movements, increase name recognition and involvement with this song. This can go on for as long as needed or simply be a quick attention-getter.

Take turns making funny faces or movements with your bodies.

As a toddler, Joy is on the move and she only wants to move fast! Her PHYSICAL branch is growing like a weed. It's hard to keep up with her.

PHYSICAL DEVELOPMENT AND ONE-YEAR-OLDS

They are mastering their basic movements now and really getting a move on. Remember when they stayed in the same place you put them when you went to the bathroom? Those days are gone forever. Now they are cruising, walking, climbing, running, falling, and dancing all over the place. They are also getting into everything and figuring out how to get into or out of things. Don't forget to use those buckles when in a high chair, car seat, or a stroller because they turn into little Houdini magicians when they are determined enough or unsupervised. You will also want to keep plenty of water and healthy food on demand. Growth spurts are unpredictable, yet certain, so be ready.

PHYSICAL ACTIVITIES AND EXAMPLES

It's all about sensory with ice cube exploration, snow, rocks, water, leaves, flowers, sticks, dirt, mud, suds, paint, feathers, torn paper, bubble wrap, cornmeal, flour, uncooked rice, etc.

Enjoy walking with and without shoes. Practice with sandals, boots, and moccasins too.

Provide different textured foods to try with a variety of flavors and tools.

Rolling cars down a ramp, throwing bean bags into a basket, kicking a ball on the grass, popping bubbles with a fly swatter, stomping tape on the ground, jumping on a mat, crawling through a tunnel are all ways to get their bodies moving with a focus, using tools in a purposeful way.

SPEND YOUR TIME ON PURPOSE

Toddlers need physical challenges as well as daily inside and outside experiences. They need to play with their big muscles as well as strengthen their fine motor skills and finger muscles. Don't just shuffle them from caregiving needs to caregiving needs. Teaching happens in the process of doing. Look for, create, and take advantage of those teachable moments happening throughout their days. Count how many steps from the door to the car, or stop and listen to the birds singing in the morning. Take the moments to be present and give attention to the little things. You will find that time flies rapidly. Seize the day. Carpe diem!!!

Use their five senses to enhance their environment. Give them interesting things to look at, different textures to feel, unique smells and foods to experience, and sounds to stimulate their growth and development.

TEACHER JOY'S BOOKSHELF

Quick as a Cricket by Audrey and Don Wood illustrate all of the empowering things we can be, and *Blueberries for Sal* by Robert McCloskey and *Snowmen At Night* by Caralyn Buehner are funny reads.

TEACHER JOY'S SONGBOOK

TEDDY BEAR, TEDDY BEAR

This body movement song gives instructions for moving bodies. Do some of the same movements every time but also add in some fun ones, teaching vocabulary or giving them directions on where to go next. It keeps kiddos paying attention when you mix it up.

As a two-year-old, Joy loves to go on outings! She goes to the store and to the zoo. She meets new people and animals. She has playdates with friends and is growing strong SOCIALLY.

SOCIAL DEVELOPMENT AND TWO-YEAR-OLDS

At this age, you are able to start to practice social skills such as cooperation or sharing toys and space. This is a learning process, so have patience and coach clearly and repetitively with simple phrases like, "feet on the ground for safety," or "gentle touches with your hands." Make sure to tell them the action you want them to do instead of barking "no" or "stop it" all the time. You are laying the foundation for future independent success. Watching littles play together without butting in and taking over to solve their problems is sometimes a challenge. If you do, it robs them of the skill practice they need. Try coaching them instead.

SOCIAL ACTIVITIES AND EXAMPLES

Baby dolls and baby accessories increase social role-playing and skills.

Play with friends older, younger, and the same age is great. Look for Mommy and Me playgroups, music classes, open gym play, and early learning opportunities. Make friends with parents.

Seek out friends of diverse color, language, physical or mental ability, ages, and genders.

Two-year-old kiddos can be sassy. Do not give into the demands or accept whining instead of words. Simply request the right way as a matter of fact, "I can't understand what you are trying to say. Try again with kind words and a respectful tone."

TERRIBLE TO TERRICIC TWOS

Temper tantrums can and will happen at some point, as they are discovering their desires and understanding they have social superpowers. Your response is vital. First, try to prevent, redirect, or defuse with humor. If that is unsuccessful, give them the safe space to let their emotions out and accept that sometimes we don't get what we want. They may have to cry outside of the restaurant or hit a pillow or blow it out and try it again when they are ready.

Think about your toddler's daily routine and avoid challenges like the grocery store when they are tired and hungry, or set up for success with a snack and a list. If they have a job or something in their hands to keep them busy, you are avoiding those pitfalls or bad habits like handing them cartoons on a digital device.

TEACHER JOY'S BOOKSHELF

The Selfish Crocodile by Faustin Charles teaches understanding and *The Little Blue Truck* by Alice Schertle and *Chester's Way* by Kevin Henkes all teach kindness, helpfulness, and friendship-building skills.

TEACHER JOY'S SONGBOOK

SHAKE A FRIEND'S HAND

Repeat this song, using a new action each time. Examples: Give a high five, rub a friend's back, or give a good hug. Sway or dance around as you sing the la-la part.

Brainstorm kind touches and model how you want them to do it as you sing. Enhance the handshake verse by putting some glitter on your hands to represent germs and see how they are spread before you wash hands after the song.

Joy is forming words and expressing her emotions by saying how she feels. Sometimes she feels very quiet and likes to whisper and snuggle her pup. Her EMOTIONAL branch is hanging heavy.

EMOTIONAL DEVELOPMENT AND TWO-YEAR-OLDS

Don't avoid emotions. Work through them instead. Give the child ownership of what they feel and time to practice gaining control. Offer as much love, guidance, and understanding as you can. Sometimes it can feel like sociological warfare. Don't let hungry or tired children bully you. Instead give them the space, time, and calming skills to get past the emotional freak outs. They will sometimes look for the opportunity and explode in social settings, or scream at the top of their lungs at the library to try and get their wants fulfilled. Respond kindly, calmly, and swiftly and remove them from the space with a matter-of-fact attitude, "Oh man, you are showing me that you cannot come to the store with me today. We can try again tomorrow when you can calm yourself." You need to follow through and be consistent to ensure they don't start a habit.

EMOTIONAL ACTIVITIES AND EXAMPLES

Create a cozy space in your home or their room to go to when they need to calm down with soft pillows, stuffed animals, and board books to look at. Littles need alone time too.

You can make cool spaces under tables and blanket forts.

Guided meditation, soothing music, massage, affirmations, and reading books about mindset are powerful tools and skills to develop positive habits early on.

Channel aggression by giving it an acceptable outlet. Physical energy needs a place to go.

DEVELOP ROUTINES FOR THE WIN!

Whether it's a morning routine to get out the door on time, a naptime routine to prepare for a successful evening, or a bedtime routine to remain sane, schedules are good. The exact time isn't the essential part; it's the series of events in order. Write it down. Create a visual schedule with your child on a poster board and hang it on their door. This prevents power struggles and gives them a point of reference. Make it fun and interactive. Have special rituals, like one kiss on each finger to say goodnight, jump and spin three times when your shoes are on, etc. Give choices when you can (which toothbrush, pajamas, or bedtime story?), so it is less of a power struggle when you can't give them a choice.

TEACHER JOY'S BOOKSHELF

The Way I Feel and *The Way I Act* by Janan Cain are so much fun to introduce and practice emotions. *Catching the Moon* by Crystal Hubbard encourages girl empowerment and determination.

TEACHER JOY'S SONGBOOK

FIVE LITTLE HOT DOGS SONG

This surprise-you song is a fun way to engage kids with a little startle or get a sensitive child accustomed to loud noises in a fun and involved way. It is also a good song to show a story taking place, and you can discuss washing hands, kitchen safety, and likes and dislikes. Continue to repeat counting down to zero, counting your fingers, and doing the math each time.

Joy's COGNITIVE skills are in full swing now. When she goes to new places or touches different things, her mind grows in leaps and bounds. Sometimes she talks using her own language where only she knows what she is saying.

COGNITIVE DEVELOPMENT AND TWO-YEAR-OLDS

This is when all of that talking to your baby pays off! They start talking back and you get to discover what they really know, how they think, and what they want. They will repeat after you. They can answer questions and argue for their point. This is a magical time of incredible growth for their brain and personality. It all comes alive. They are more interested in the world around them, identifying shapes, colors, numbers, and animals, so don't hold back. Talk about different people, industries, geography, and experiences. Introduce new words daily.

COGNITIVE ACTIVITIES AND EXAMPLES

Find cause and effect activities such as spraying with spray bottles, using pipettes or turkey basters to move colored water, and watching absorption or gravity in action on purpose.

Paint using unique tools like balloons, old toothbrushes, sponges, utensils, sticks, or toy cars.

Do not use flash cards, video games, or cartoons to teach your child. Hands-on, engaged interaction is what young children need. Give them your time and fun experiences!

Go out and see the world. Mother nature is a remarkable teacher and there is so much to experience. Go watch a mechanic, visit the library, and attend farmers markets and stores.

FIERCLY INDEPENDENT

Stop doing everything for them. This is the time for them to build independent skills and, one of the most important things ever, problem-solving skills!

To enhance this lesson and give them practice, come at any challenge as a mystery to solve. "Oh no! We have a missing shoe! Whatever are we going to do?" and let them put their thinking caps on and save the day with their clever problem-solving.

Any time you can make a game out of life or a fun activity or a spunky song, they engage and are able to receive the planned or spontaneous lesson. Look for those teachable moments.

Give them jobs they can do independently, like setting the table, putting clothes away, or cleaning up their things.

TEACHER JOY'S BOOKSHELF

Brown Bear, Brown Bear, What Do You See by Bill Martin, Jr. is one to read over and over again. *Freight Train* by Donald Crews teaches colors and train cars, and *The Paper Bag Princess* by Robert Munsch is all about being clever.

TEACHER JOY'S SONGBOOK

ZOOM-ZOOM-ZOOM

There is so much going on in this awesome song: upbeat, repeated words, counting down numbers, excitement for the blast-off, creative brainstorming, rhyming, and outer space concepts. And it's downright fun to sing. For each verse, you can create a different rhyme and destination: far-star, fun-sun, loud-cloud, etc. Think of more destinations together with the kiddos.

Two-year-old Joy sings, dances, and listens to books read to her, and it opens her imagination and helps her grow CREATIVE branches. She listens to music at home and different music at her grandma's home, which form even more branches.

CREATIVE DEVELOPMENT AND TWO-YEAR-OLDS

What a perfect time in life! They are really unfolding their personalities and character now. In creating their own ideas, enjoying their play, and coming up with the funniest games, life is so full. They have wide-open wonder and they are great teachers for us to remember to embrace our silly, childlike side and look at things from their point of view. Have an incredible amount of patience with them at this time because it is in the process that they are growing. Raising a great, well-rounded person takes time and intention. Truly, this age is notorious for not walking the straight path, but rather meandering down a looping trail. Enrich their days with opportunities to enjoy the scenery without rushing them along. Get down on their level and do your best to see what they see.

CREATIVE ACTIVITIES AND EXAMPLES

Find creative picture books to read and discuss. Look at the pictures and talk about the details.

Listen to music, dance crazy, play with musical instruments, and act out familiar stories.

Use all of the dramatic play toys! Pretend play is in full swing now. They just need props to bring their imaginations to life: empty box grocery store, a tool set, camping supplies, costumes, medical supplies, etc.

Write the words they use to describe their drawings and mark it with a date.

ASK OPEN-ENDED QUESTIONS

"Why do you think that happened?" "Where do you think that bee is flying to?" "What do you think that sound could be?" "I don't know. What do you think?"

When you ask a child an open-ended question, it gets their wheels turning to create an answer. This method opens their thinking and stimulates their own creativity and flow.

Look for chances to ask them questions they can answer any way they want. Life can be so concrete, and without being purposeful like this, their days can be filled with boundaries and directive must-do actions, which only teaches them to be diligent and obedient, not to think for themselves. Young children need the chance to figure things out on their own.

TEACHER JOY'S BOOKSHELF

Chicka Chicka Boom Boom by Bill Martin, Jr. and John Archambault, and *Jamberry* by Bruce Degen are books to read with a beat. *How I Became a Pirate* by Melinda Long is as fun for the reader as it is for the kids.

TEACHER JOY'S SONGBOOK

SHAKE YOUR SILLIES OUT

This fun, open-ended movement song is great for releasing energy before expecting young children to sit for a while, or when you are transitioning to outside play and you need to focus their energy to move together safely. Do the motions as you sing the song and change them each time you sing. Be creative and silly. Examples: Jump your jiggles, sleep your sleepers, stretch your stretchers, march your marchers, giggle your giggles.

Joy's movement is getting easier, and she can do more things as her body grows. She has mastered getting around and her PHYSICAL branches are strong enough to climb on.

PHYSICAL DEVELOPMENT AND TWO-YEAR-OLDS

Two-year-old kiddos need to move and explore both their bodies and their environments. Every possible chance, try to set up physical challenges for them: a pile of pillows to mount, a box to climb in and out, an obstacle course of around, over, under and through challenges. As they get older, you can increase the challenge. Teach different physical commands such as hop, run, walk, and crawl, and then add crazy ones on there like tippy toes, robot walk, crab crawl, or belly slither to increase their capabilities and interests. You can set yourself up for a successful naptime or calm dinner if you get their energy out first.

PHYSICAL ACTIVITIES AND EXAMPLES

Teach and practice yoga and stretching as well as mindful breathing and quiet times.

Dress-up clothes promote self-help and skill-building when they put clothes on by themselves.

Picking up small toys with tongs or a spatula, using different body parts like elbows, increases muscle control.

Set up an obstacle course using household furniture, and do it with them, explaining how you are moving your body as you go, "I am hopping on one foot around the table..."

Manipulatives such as string beads, bristle blocks, Duplo blocks, geo boards, gears, simple jigsaw puzzles, dominoes, bunny builders, and peg boards are great for practicing fine motor skills.

Provide hard clay, add texture to playdough, mix dirt for mud pies, fill balloons with pebbles, and give them sandpaper and rough-cut wood to sand to feel different textiles.

POTTY-TRAINING

Please do not over-complicate potty training. The goal of potty training isn't just for them to go to the bathroom on the toilet upon request; it is to make sure they can do all of the potty-training steps completely and independently. You only have a short time in their lives to be in the bathroom with them to make sure they know how to wipe all of the poo away before pulling their pants back up. Don't do it for them and take away their chance to practice with supervision.

The right time to start potty-training is when they are interested, capable of doing it by themselves, and not in a stressful life moment. Commit all the way and be consistent.

TEACHER JOY'S BOOKSHELF

Froggy Gets Dressed by Jonathan London includes unique sounds to read and *Whistle for Willie* by Ezra Jack Keats is a book about perseverance when learning a new skill.

TEACHER JOY'S SONGBOOK

5 THINGS CHANT

Create smoother transitions by using this simple chant consistently when going from outdoors to inside. It gathers a group of kids with non-direct cues, engages music with movement, and teaches body parts, actions, and number recognition and placement. Oh, and getting off any sand, dirt, snow, or water before going inside.

Joy gets together with her friends every week. She is learning at preschool with a teacher now. She likes learning how to be a good friend. SOCIALLY, her development is just getting stronger.

SOCIAL DEVELOPMENT AND THREE-YEAR-OLDS

This carefree, fun-loving age is what I would define as bliss. They have a life free of responsibilities and knowledge of global current events, and they can make instant friends with anyone they meet. Enjoy buckets of giggles together, for these are the days you will look back on and remember when you are both old. Build memories and a positive inner voice for them in the future. Model, encourage, and assist them in asking questions, being curious socially, and being honest and kind. Being a good friend takes effort and intention. Make sure they see examples of adult friends having a good time together too.

SOCIAL ACTIVITIES AND EXAMPLES

Role-play and act out social examples of conversation and share ideas with one another during play. Use props and imaginary tools to enhance your play.

Embrace imaginary friends. They won't be around forever, so let them be a part of life now and use them to practice being considerate. A lovie can be a good stand-in too.

Sharing space, time, and materials with others can provide a chance for taking turns, waiting practices, and communication skills. Expect and model the respectful language.

Practice self-image by drawing portraits, letter and body tracing, or taking pictures.

THREE-NAGER SOAP OPERAS

They will tattle on all of their friends, even if they weren't involved. They will want to talk all about it, like the town gossip. You will undoubtedly hear who hit who, took a toy, or said a bad word. They also sometimes exaggerate the truth or outright lie, so be clear now about honesty and require truthfulness.

They want to know what others are thinking and feeling. This is where they learn empathy, respect, communication, kindness, and friendship-building skills. Talk about what happened with their friends, dissect their social encounters, and discuss how else they can respond to challenges. You are investing in your connection when they are teenagers. You want them to feel free, safe, and comfortable talking to you now, so they get in the habit and continue naturally.

TEACHER JOY'S BOOKSHELF

A Chair for My Mother by Vera B. Williams and *The Rainbow Fish* by Marcus Pfister are about generosity and sharing. *A Color of His Own, Swimmy,* and *Little Blue and Little Yellow* by Leo Lionni are all books about friendship and differences.

TEACHER JOY'S SONGBOOK

UNCLE JESSE

Build it up in the beginning with a story about a friend Jesse who only has so much room in his horse and buggy but loves friends and dancing, so he narrows down who comes with him by selecting different attributes like age, hair color, what they are wearing, or letters their names start with. Change the characteristic or what they are wearing each time you sing a round.

Three-year-old Joy is independent! She can and wants to do everything all by herself. When she masters something that is hard, she beams with pride. Her family calls her cranky when she is tired and that makes her angry. She is getting a lot of chances to grow her EMOTIONAL branches.

EMOTIONAL DEVELOPMENT AND THREE-YEAR-OLDS

Providing an environment where they are safe to make mistakes, learn from their actions, and ask questions will help create self-confidence. Feeling nervous about new experiences is natural, and there are ways you can make a positive learning opportunity out of their anxiety. First, honor and accept their feelings. Offer some adjectives to help them label what they feel. Then practice some tools like explaining what to expect. Break it down into simple steps, positive visualizations, or a security item or thought. When there is a consistent reaction with few exceptions, they learn to trust your reactions and also learn flexibility if you explain along the way. Remember, they are looking at you for the reassurance during this learning time.

EMOTIONAL ACTIVITIES AND EXAMPLES

Lovie stuffed animals can aid in free snuggles or quiet whispers when needed.

Mindset practices done together form lifelong positive habits of meditation and deep breathing and gaining control of wild and untamed emotions.

Catch them doing good things, celebrate natural kindness, and allow reflection time to bask in the pride of making good choices. Speak highly about them in front of them.

Research and practice *The Five Love Languages* to shower them with love in every way.

Set the stage for being brave. Create some monster spray and add a night light or soft music.

AUTONOMY

The goal is to empower them with the gift of autonomy and making the right decisions without being told. There will come a time when they are faced with making a good or bad choice, and by building their autonomy, you increase confidence that they will make the right one. This skill is taught right now, by giving them freedom to take the risks and learn from the consequences while they are still supervised and stopped before it becomes unsafe or harmful. Use those moments where they are close to the edge of a boundary to discuss what could happen and ask those open-ended questions, so they are able to do the critical thinking.

TEACHER JOY'S BOOKSHELF

The Kissing Hand by Audrey Penn is about overcoming feeling anxious, and *In My Heart* by Jo Witek is a sweet and encouraging book. *The Feelings Book* and *It's Okay to be Different* by Todd Parr and *The Story of Ferdinand* by Munro Leaf are fun and simple to read.

TEACHER JOY'S SONGBOOK

THE BANANA SONG

This is a high-energy movement song that ends with screaming and running around crazy! There is a smart way to use this song when the kids need something unexpected and wild. It's great to do in a big yard or running space, or to teach spatial awareness and caution while moving fast.

Joy loves learning! She wants to know her colors and the names of every animal. She counts everything she sees, and her mind seems to zoom like a rocket all of the time. She is supporting her COGNITIVE thinking with each new idea she considers or question she asks.

COGNITIVE DEVELOPMENT AND THREE-YEAR-OLDS

Smart little three-year-old's need a challenge, a problem to solve or something that needs to be explored, to collect important data to be analyzed. They are walking, talking, tiny scientists and should be provided with a rich playground of experiences to build their cognitive brain. Follow their lead and interests to dive deeper into understanding and give quality time to research and discovery. Learning is best done through hands-on experiences outside of a desk or screen to create the mental connections needed to be successful in life. The object of teaching is not filling their minds, but rather sparking a love of learning.

COGNITIVE ACTIVITIES AND EXAMPLES

Utilize STEM activities, problem-solving with open-ended questions, and creatively structured engineering toys and loose parts to construct whatever they can come up with.

Explore the museums, visit the library, watch a game or a race from the sidelines, visit petting zoos and aquariums, and discuss their observations and answer their questions.

Go on bug hunts, research and build habitats, purchase worms and lady bugs from the hardware store. Release the ladybugs into a garden and use worm castings to nourish it.

Care for a family pet or visit a local animal shelter to observe and interact with animals.

Play with different sensory bins full of dry beans, rice, birdseed, shaving cream, and such.

FACILITATING PLANNED ACTIVITIES AND EMERGENT CURRICULUM

With a purposefully-designed environment, children will naturally practice scientific inquiry, build cognitive skills, and learn during play. These environments inspire the enjoyable balance between planned and spontaneous activities or lessons.

Adult-facilitated but CHILD-LED activities plant, water, and fertilize seeds of interest. Start by offering limited choices and add more of what draws them. Jump deeper into the areas they are interested in and plan out ways to deepen their understanding. When they lose interest or become more interested in something different, follow their new interests and make a new plan accordingly.

TEACHER JOY'S BOOKSHELF

Too Much Noise by Ann McGovern and *Wilfred Gordan McDonald Partridge* by Mem Fox are magnificent books. The classic *Cat in the Hat* by Dr. Seuss is full of rhyming words.

TEACHER JOY'S SONGBOOK

SWEET POTATO SOUP

There are loads of learning opportunities with this song. Start with lap-slapping and clapping to a beat. Then let kids take turns saying what food they want to add and how much, count and chop it all up with imaginary movements, and stir it up. Then move on to the next child or take turns with parents. To end, taste the soup and recall all of the ingredients.

Pretend play is so much fun for Joy the preschooler. She acts out stories and dresses up like a jungle beast and has tea parties with her dog. She loves to paint with lots of colors. This all builds more CREATIVE branches.

CREATIVE DEVELOPMENT AND THREE-YEAR-OLDS

The life of a three-year-old should be magical and happy. Add whimsy whenever you can. Empower individualism and inspire them to form their own opinion. Let them dress themselves, pick out what they want from a menu, and choose the books to read or songs to sing. This blossoming of their spirit should be cultivated. Fill in their curiosity about places they haven't been by looking at books, videos, and pictures and describing faraway places like the jungle, forest, island beach, under the sea, or outer space. Have fun investigating and imagining what it would be like to go to each of these places and then visit places you can.

CREATIVE ACTIVITIES AND EXAMPLES

Attend plays and concerts to inspire them and give them practice being in an audience.

Make a backdrop or scenery for their own performances. Add costumes or microphones and a supporting cast as needed. Then record this keepsake for their kids to watch.

Hide fun treasures for kids to find in high-sensory locations to foster a sense of excitement and curiosity.

Provide water ways in the dirt to create dams. Practice sinking and floating, or make mud.

Dance in the rain, build a snowman or a sand castle, jump in a pile of leaves, melt ice on the sidewalk, paint outside with water and watch it disappear, or leave water out and watch it freeze. Mother nature is so cool and supplies so many learning opportunities.

THE PROCESS IN WHICH WE LEARN

Life is messy and unpredictable, and so is a three-year-old's creative process!

My best advice for you is, "Let there be mess!" Outside with a wet towel close by and in play clothes and at play time. If young children are given the opportunity to have that outlet, they will thrive creatively. However, that does not mean you can't be smart about it. Plan it and plan for the pitfalls too. Be prepared and have the tools you need to fit your personal comfort level.

Redirect those wild dance parties to the play area. Keep mud outside and take your shoes off before you come back inside. Bring them to early learning classrooms where they can have access to more sensory, dramatic play, and art.

It is the process, not the product, of learning that matters most.

TEACHER JOY'S BOOKSHELF

Joseph Had a Little Overcoat by Simms Taback teaches that you can always make something out of nothing by reusing it. *Not a Box* by Antoinette Portis is all about imagination. *Miss Rumphius* by Barbara Cooney inspires kids to make the world a beautiful place.

TEACHER JOY'S SONGBOOK

ICKY STICKY BUBBLE GUM

This song is great for being silly, recognizing body parts, repeating words and verses, telling a story, and teaching handwashing. Start by sparking the imagination and giving out pretend gumballs, letting kids decide their color, put them in their mouths, describe the flavor, and blow up a bubble that pops as you start the song.

Joy has learned to write her name and she just can't stop. She draws picture after picture just to practice her fine motor skills, strengthening her finger muscles and growing her PHYSICAL branch.

PHYSICAL DEVELOPMENT AND THREE-YEAR-OLDS

They can do it! All by themselves! They are capable and driven to be independent. Empower them with learning their name, recognizing it, spelling it, and even writing it. Each child is unique with different talents at different times, so celebrate where your child is at each stage without pressure. Just have fun. Practice writing skills as it follows their interest, but keep it available and encouraged. The more they draw, the more you will see their control and intention with their pictures. Celebrate and write the things they see and say to honor their process of growth.

PHYSICAL ACTIVITIES AND EXAMPLES

Experiment with new, healthy fruits and vegetables and foods from different origins and restaurants. Diversify their palate through exposure and encouragement.

Play with ride-on toys: big wheels, four-wheelers, scooters, bikes, skateboards, or skates.

Go on a walk as often as possible, around the block or on a nature hike. Just go out and explore the world and get their bodies moving and seeing things out in nature.

Practice repetitive motion activities like stamping, hammering, pushing and pulling toys, sanding, painting, sidewalk chalking, parachute playing, jump roping, and swinging.

HEALTHY HABITS AND HYGIENE

A regular practice of taking care of your business provides long-lasting benefits. Make sure they know how to wash their hands with warm water, scrubbing all of their parts with soap, floss their teeth, and brush their hair. They need interaction and encouragement to gain these skills. This is the time to teach healthy life skills and how to be responsible for keeping their bodies clean. Keeping germs at bay keeps it healthy, and caring for our body keeps it in good working condition.

Sweets should be limited or nonexistent with young children and never used as a reward to prevent future habits such as overeating, or outcomes such as illness, obesity, or addiction. Instead provide other forms of praise or a healthier alternative.

TEACHER JOY'S BOOKSHELF

Parts and More Parts by Tedd Arnold are funny books about bodies and *Chrysanthemum* by Kevin Henkes is a book about having a cool name and being proud of it. *The Song and Dance Man* by Karen Ackerman is about aging and memory.

TEACHER JOY'S SONGBOOK

BUTTON FACTORY

How many body parts can you move at once? Right arm, left arm, right and left legs, head, tongue, and maybe even blink your eyes too! Use this song to teach boundaries, multiple movements, right versus left, body parts, balance, and energy-releasing. You will have to model movements for littles and follow the lead of bigs when teaching to allow for age-appropriate comprehension.

Joy is four years old now and she is the best friend to all of her friends. She is also an excellent helper with her neighbors and teachers. She is always planning a trip to visit someone far away, building lots of SOCIAL branches.

SOCIAL DEVELOPMENT AND FOUR-YEAR-OLDS

Now you can finally have some good two-way conversations. Their social understanding of the world is deeper and you can do cool things like discuss your family values and beliefs, write your family story, illustrate your family tree, send letters and pictures to family and friends that live far away, and video call. Build their social circles outside their immediate world. You can reason with, negotiate, and debate topics of interest. Look for a win-win or no-deal situation where you keep everyone's best interests in mind when making decisions.

SOCIAL ACTIVITIES AND EXAMPLES

Look out for other parents and support them. Offer your best advice when asked and problem-solve together when you don't have a good answer.

Set up household or classroom chores and responsibilities to care for their environment.

Have a party! Find any reason for a celebration. It could be a holiday or just Taco Tuesday!

Meet up with friends for a bike ride, hike, swim, walk, wall climb, or community event.

Set up a sleepover or a playdate with friends at each other's homes or a planned phone call. Connect with your children's friends, teachers, and caregivers.

BEST FRIENDS AND BULLIES

Leadership, respect, and communication skills are developed while forming, failing, and fixing relationships with friends and family members. There are some things you can do now to support marvelous outcomes in the future. Avoid sarcasm and teasing or picking on each other at home. Socially coach alongside sibling rivalry with love and respect. Or sit down at a peace table and take turns sharing feelings for children to feel heard.

Competition for some kiddos is natural and if you have one, make sure to give them a healthy outlook and understanding about when and where is the time for competing.

When kids are intentionally mean, sneaky, or defiant, address it and be respectfully clear with a no tolerance expectation.

TEACHER JOY'S BOOKSHELF

Have You Filled a Bucket Today by Carol McCloud Johnson and *Somebody Loves You Mister Hatch* by Eileen Spinelli and *A Sick Day for Amos Mcgee* by Philip C. Stead are all fantastic books about kindness. *The Day You Begin* by Jaqueline Woodson is about finding courage.

TEACHER JOY'S SONGBOOK

JUMP JIM JOE

Add a musical instrument like a drum, rhythm sticks, or even clapping to keep the beat and steady energy of this dance-around song.

Dancing with a partner is a different skill than dancing alone, and a large group with a faster pace adds even more social navigation.

There are so many emotions. Joy tries them all on each day, and sometimes just to herself in front of the mirror. Other people's emotions are very interesting too. She likes to make her friends laugh when they are sad so they can both be happy. EMOTIONALLY, she is developing beautifully.

EMOTIONAL DEVELOPMENT AND FOUR-YEAR-OLDS

Life should be full of laughter and lightheartedness, but sometimes tragedy strikes: friends move away or death, divorce, and disaster happen. There are so many extreme and confusing mental and emotional reactions. Different people process and express grief differently, and children do too. Provide them with honest answers, time to process, physical affection and nurturing, and an outlet for their energy and feelings. Reassure each other and do activities that bring everyone joy. There are times when they will face fear and they need to know what to do or who to talk to when they need help. Prepare them with a plan and trustworthy people.

EMOTIONAL ACTIVITIES AND EXAMPLES

Create a family emergency plan and practice to build confidence. Teach them emergency numbers, their address, and whole names. Discuss a back-up plan. Knowledge is power.

Look for body language and address when things look or feel out-of-sorts.

Avoid public humiliation. This can leave lasting negative impact on their self-confidence.

Practice and model respect, recognition, acceptance, appreciation, and praise for what people do around you and in front of your child, especially in your family.

Practice daily affirmations, giving each other compliments and valuing acts of service.

Don't watch the news when the children are around. Filter their media intake.

GOAL-SETTING SKILLS AND DREAMING

We want our kids to grow up to be anything they can imagine, including successful and fulfilled. Achieving those dreams starts in early childhood. Goal-setting can be fun when building toward something special, including working and saving money for a desired item. These are all positive ways to build anticipation and reach gratification. Visual aids like tracking progress on a chart support this habit.

Bribery disempowers children in the long run. They are not building anticipation; they are forming expectation. Giving them an instant reward for expected behavior, based on a threat or a dangled carrot, robs them of the lesson and devalues the desired object. The benefit of not giving into the moment pays off, so stay strong and consistent.

TEACHER JOY'S BOOKSHELF

The One, The Only Magnificent Me by Dan Haseltine is about encouragement and feeling proud and *Ruby Finds a Worry* by Tom Percival and *Belly Breathe* by Leslie Kimmelman teach calming tools.

TEACHER JOY'S SONGBOOK

THE BUMBLE BEE FLEW OUT OF THE TREE

This song is perfect for rhyming and body part identification as well as building anticipation. It's a favorite to goof around with and tickle your own child, or you can see if a student can guess where the rhyming part is while the bee is buzzing nearby without touching them.

What if I miss you?
Why don't turtles fly?
How do you play the flute?
family photos
COGNITIVE
CREATIVE
EMOTIONAL
PHYSICAL
SOCIAL
WORLD RECORDS
YELLOW-STONE REUNION
JOY
When can I go swimming?
Who is my cousin?
With a very busy mind at work, Joy's COGNITIVE branch stretches tall. She wants to know why things are the way they are and asks a lot of questions. Her mind thinks about places she has only heard about in stories and things she has never seen. She is forming her dreams and goals of things she wants to do when she grows up.

COGNITIVE DEVELOPMENT AND FOUR-YEAR-OLDS

These tenacious thinkers want to suck all of your knowledge right out of you. Acknowledge their interests and strengthen their understanding by giving them a ton of facts and experimental outlets. Most importantly, teach them how to find their own answers. That is true empowerment. In a world where anything we can dream up can be defined for us at the tip of our fingers and technology is moving rapidly through our existence, we don't know what they will see in their lifetime, but it will be a lot.

COGNITIVE ACTIVITIES AND EXAMPLES

Go on a bear hunt and problem-solve what to do, what to bring, and how to overcome obstacles.

Teach and practice composting, recycling, conservation, and how to take care of mother earth. If we teach our kids, then they will teach their kids and so on.

Build catapults and pulleys. Use pumps, balance scales, and ramps to explore simple mechanics.

Introduce and experiment with complex thinking like volume, density, velocity, and impact.

ASKING AND ANSWERING WHY

Studies have shown that a four-year-old asks as many as 200 to 300 questions in a single day!

How do you answer every one of them? Use each time as a learning opportunity, ask them what they think, answer with honesty and in simple to grasp concepts. Make it a researching opportunity and look it up, visit the library, or go ask a specialist.

There will come a time, and it is okay to say, "I'm just not sure" or "go ask your father."

We want to foster curiosity and engage in conversation but sometimes we need a break. Challenge them in other ways, engage them in a physical task or occupy their mouth with a different activity like humming or whistling instead of getting frustrated. We do not want to stifle their curiosity and sometimes the right answer is to think about it and discuss it later or have a designated talking time or place.

TEACHER JOY'S BOOKSHELF

Leo the Late Bloomer by Robert Kraus is about having patience, and *Stellaluna* by Janell Cannon is a remarkable book. *Mouse Paint* or *Mouse Count* by Ellen Stoll Walsh makes learning fun.

TEACHER JOY'S SONGBOOK

SLIPPERY FISH

Teach different sea life animals, what they do, and how they eat. This song is great as an interactive flannel board showing the scale of the sea creatures fitting inside one another. The whale being the biggest, he burps at the end (kids love that part) and then he says "excuse me" in a deep whale voice.

CREATIVELY, Joy is in full blossom. Her ideas and stories flow like water. Her parents write down the creative thoughts as she dictates them. Together, they have made a book of her ideas. She loves to read her book to her class, and now the whole class is going to make one.

CREATIVE DEVELOPMENT AND FOUR-YEAR-OLDS

Inspire greatness by believing in them and their process of learning and becoming their best selves. You can distract them from harmful influences and attract them to positive learning by consistently investing time, energy, and purpose into their surroundings. Rotate toys and learning tools through their play space. Seek out great early learning classrooms and high-quality childcare experiences. Congratulate yourself for reading this book and continue to look for ways to enhance their development.

CREATIVE ACTIVITIES AND EXAMPLES

Create an art station stocked with scrap paper, glue sticks, crayons, markers, stencils, feathers, glitter, nature pieces, yarn, hole punch, tape, paper strips, and rounded scissors. (Hair grows back.)

Trains and tracks, cars, trucks, play people and play animal figures, dinosaurs and bugs are fun toys.

Sketch their tile, tangram, or block creations, or draw one for them to try and duplicate.

Become inventors and create solutions to everyday problems or make the world better.

Read tons of books, good quality storybooks, that expand their thinking.

UNADULTERATED IMAGINATION

Make your own book of ideas. Ask children open-ended questions about what to do when they are feeling lonely, scared, bored, or happy. Maybe someone you love is sick or sad. Make up your own questions to fit your needs. Have a blank paper and a pencil available and write down the question and the response in quotations. Provide few prompts and encourage them say anything they want and even add a picture to illustrate their thoughts.

Regular journaling and dictation of stories builds their creativity and understanding and validates their creative thinking.

Record videos and take pictures of their creative expressions and display their artwork with pride and honor. Send extras or outdated art to distant friends. Celebrate making pictures for the ill or elderly as an act of kindness to make them happy.

TEACHER JOY'S BOOKSHELF

If... by Sarah Perry and *Maybe* by Kobi Yamada build imagination. *Seven Blind Mice* by Ed Young teaches perspective and *Harold and The Purple Crayon* by Crockett Johnson is great for creative drawing. *Islandborn* by Junot Diaz is about visualizing and interpretation.

TEACHER JOY'S SONGBOOK

DON'T THROW YOUR JUNK

Ask kids what they think would be awful to find in their backyard and use their suggestions. Sing about each one and add each new one to the end after repeating each answer already used. It is interesting to hear what they think is disgusting, and it builds recall because of the gross stuff shared. See how many you can do before you start forgetting what has been said.

What a crazy girl Joy can be sometimes! When she and Bo turn the music up loud and get dancing, they really go wild. Her body is a PHYSICAL masterpiece. She eats healthy food and gets good sleep and keeps moving all of her parts to build strong muscles.

PHYSICAL DEVELOPMENT AND FOUR-YEAR-OLDS

Regular exercise, stretching, yoga, and movement are essential to a child's healthy growth. Getting enough good sleep in a safe and clean space, free of clutter, noise, and chaos are a must. Having access to clean water and healthy foods, prepared and always available, is what each child needs for their bodies to grow. Teach them to care for themselves, thank those who provide for them, and tend to each other and their environments. It will build lasting health and well-being and instill responsibility.

ACTIVITIES AND EXAMPLES

Do morning calisthenics, counting your movements as you exercise. Do jumping jacks, push-ups, sit-ups, high kicks, one-foot hopping, up-down bends, squats, dance moves, etc. to mix it up.

Eat healthy and drink plenty of water, explaining the benefits.

Plant a garden, visit farms, attend farmers markets, and go to the grocery stores to show them where food comes from and appreciate the farmers' and orchardists' hard work.

Join in organized team sports in your community and watch local teams play. Attend a dance class or gymnastics class to learn new movements and see others move.

CALCULATED RISK-TAKING

Have a first aid kit, ice packs, and Band-Aids. Sometimes lessons can hurt. There are risks in life, and they can be quite successful taking risks as adults if we let them learn how to calculate those risks when they are young and let them hone in on their personal prevention skills.

Don't put them in a bubble or fly a helicopter above them. Life is meant to be lived and experienced without fear or intimidation. Conjuring up courage, following curiosity, or testing cause and effect can all be great lessons that can also result in scars, good stories, and maybe even possibly inspiring a kid to be a nurse when they grow up.

Remember to let kids be kids and bask in this time of enjoyment and wonder. It will soon be a memory you share as a story.

TEACHER JOY'S BOOKSHELF

A Bad Case of Stripes by David Shannon and *Tops and Bottoms* by Janet Stevens are books about clever thinking. *Those Mean Nasty Dirty Downright Disgusting But... Invisible Germs* by Judith Anne Rice illustrates germs at school.

TEACHER JOY'S SONGBOOK

TEAMS' TREE SONG

Brainstorm natural and beneficial seed coverings (mulch, soil, bunny poop, etc.) to plant while the kids get into a ball on the ground. Go through the song with the body movements of a seed growing into a large plant or tree dramatized for energy release and then slow down as the plants and "trees" fall. Repeat the song to demonstrate the cycle of life.

Joy is five years old now and, my goodness, she has grown! Her mind is ready to jump into deeper learning. Joy is starting kindergarten soon and she is SOCIALLY prepared for a big group of friends. EMOTIONALLY, she feels confident because she knows what school is like and how to have fun. COGNITIVELY, her mind is set up to learn new things and has a good foundation to build on. CREATIVELY, she is wide open to be herself and explore her interests. PHYSICALLY, she is able to take on any challenge with her strong body.

FIVE-YEAR-OLDS

This is a beautiful representation of a child's mind that is swelling with information and excitement for life. The gift of attention and consistency built the foundation for success. Now between the ages of five and eight, the natural pruning takes place. This is when the child's brain is no longer striving to connect and develop, but it is discarding unused roadways. They still have brain plasticity to learn new things for the remainder of their lives, but this special time of child development has come to an end. Thank you for contributing with love.

ACTIVITIES AND EXAMPLES

Provide a routine for their day and week, including attending a pre-k program to give them hands-on practice in a developmentally appropriate classroom.

Give them exposure and practice engaging with children their age and learning from other adults.

Visit kindergarten classrooms in the spring to know what to expect in the fall.

Value and love the early childhood educators. Being a teacher of young children is both challenging and rewarding and, above all else, extremely valuable.

KINDERGARTEN READINESS

Preparing for kindergarten has less to do with knowing their ABCs and 123s and more about being emotionally prepared to handle a structured day, understanding the expectations, and having a willingness to listen and a desire to learn. Organizational skills and the capacity to ask questions and comprehend the answer, to focus and to be self-reliant, and to think for yourself are the key ingredients for success. These are executive function skills, and the work you have been doing up until now provided the framework for their achievement.

There is more to life than elementary school, and continued growth comes from practicing the skills already learned and building on the ideas that have been formed during the early learning years.

TEACHER JOY'S BOOKSHELF

Max the Brave by Ed Vere, *The Napping House* by Audrey Wood, *Library Lion* by Michelle Knudsen, *Verdi* by Janell Cannon, and *The Rough Faced Girl* by Rafe Martin are some more of my favorite books.

TEACHER JOY'S SONGBOOK

I AM AN INSECT IN THIS LIFE

This fun insect song gets bodies up and down and around as it teaches the different parts of an insect. Repeating and counting, this fast-paced song is a fun one to sing with older kids that can keep up. Repeat and see how fast you can do the song when you need to stall and still keep kids engaged and waiting.

This is Grimm. He is Joy's very best friend, and she says that he is the smartest boy she knows. He has a physical disability and cannot do all of the same things that she can do. However, there are lots of things that he can do that she can't do, like count all the way to a thousand or read almost every book all by himself. He says his favorite one is her book of ideas.

A VARIETY OF ABILITIES

Learning from people with different abilities develops a different set of skills and can enhance their world and others with the knowledge they have gained. By combining talents, sharing ideas, and creating something together, we all benefit. Collaborate with all people, ask questions, get closer, and connect with people different than you every chance you get. We are in this together and we are stronger together. Build your team, tap your resources, and create the best version of yourself for the children you teach and raise. It is your obligation to go forth and be the change for good in this world.

INCLUSION ACTIVITIES AND EXAMPLES

Talk to all people with kindness and respect and expect children to as well. Correct them when they don't.

Visit elderly care facilities and events with people of different ages and take the time to listen.

Support programs and events that provide assistance to developmentally disabled people.

Learn about different abilities and disabilities to gain awareness and understanding. Practice living without an ability to see what skills are gained. Wear a blindfold or ear plugs, use a wheelchair or only one arm, or imagine a different ability for a day.

Get to know people that don't look or act like you and welcome them as friends.

WHAT DYSLEXIA TAUGHT ME

It took me a little longer to read and write as well as my peers, but my challenges made me driven to prove my capabilities. It forced me to find a different way than everyone else, so I could get to the comprehension. Now, that skill aids me in seeing things from many points of view. It taught me that being different is not a curse but a gift, because I am unique. Because of this mental difference, I can empathize and understand that everyone is the same and everyone is different.

People are people, developing in the same ways, and should be given the same healthy opportunities modified to fit their abilities. Love all people regardless of their abilities, skin color, language, orientation, and likes or dislikes. Just love one another.

TEACHER JOY'S BOOKSHELF

When Charley Met Emma by Amy Webb is a beautiful story of physical differences, and *Let's Go Play* by Shelby McCarthy offers tools to aid in special needs, and *Just Ask* by Sonia Sotomayor explains different special needs.

TEACHER JOY'S SONGBOOK

MAY OUR CIRCLE BE UNBROKEN

Use this song to end the school day, as a sweet lullaby at night, or even to close a dance party. Hold hands or sway alone as you sing it the first time slowly and softly, smiling at the people in the circle. Then get up and dance and sing it again but fast while clapping with high energy.

Growing up well takes a lot of help from family, friends, neighbors, teachers, and even people you don't know. When young children are given a chance to watch and do and learn in a positive environment, they can naturally grow all of their branches to become successful adults in a challenging world. The most important thing to remember is to have fun and enjoy learning.

Scan to access Teacher Joy's songs!

TEACHER JOY

It has been my pleasure spending my life's work learning from young children. They have been my very best teachers. I have had the honor of learning from excellent early childhood educators, but they could only share their understanding of young children from an adult point of view. I wanted to get deeper into the minds of our earliest learners. I wanted to see what they see from their level. To really do that, I had to get all the way down onto my belly on the ground and spend some quality time with many, many children and explore right alongside them as they experienced their firsts. I learned different things from different children over my thirty years in early learning. My own sons taught me things in the middle of frustrated sleepless nights that I could never have learned in a college forum. I understood the value of sign language with toddlers when I saw a harmonious group of fourteen toddlers communicate without adults interjecting. And there were countless lessons that I witnessed children teach the adults about listening to their needs so clearly that the adults just couldn't hear. I have made it my mission to see, not just the children's point of view. but from every position within the early learning and childcare industry. I have spent this time and energy to collect this information with the purpose of relaying it to the world in the simplest of ways to be able to reach every person interested in how children learn and how brains are developed in the first five years.

BROOKE IVEY

Creativity is a force that enriches our lives and makes us human. It can help us understand a concept and see someone else's point of view, lead us to feel an emotion, and even heal us. I dedicate my artwork to the creatives of the world. I think that can be any one of us. I hope more people can understand that it doesn't have to look perfect—that making something is good for our hearts and minds. Creativity can be a driving force behind understanding more about taking care of our Earth and each other.